Branding Brilliance

Your Blueprint to Creating & Communicating an
Irresistible Personal Brand

Thomas Allan

KFT
PUBLISHING

KFT Publishing

Paperback ISBN: 978-0-6457786-6-3

PUBLISHING

Contents

Introduction

Welcome to your journey toward creating a powerful, authentic personal brand. Whether you're an entrepreneur, a professional looking to advance your career, or an individual seeking to understand and articulate your unique value, this workbook is designed for you.

In today's digital world, personal branding is no longer optional. We all have a personal brand, whether or not we are aware of it. It's how the world sees us and can significantly impact our careers and lives. This blueprint is designed to guide you through the process of creating a personal brand that truly reflects who you are and what you stand for.

This workbook is divided into six comprehensive chapters, each focusing on a crucial aspect of personal branding. From discovering your brand and crafting your image to aligning your personal brand with your business or role, you'll find actionable advice, explanations, and exercises that will empower you to shape your brand.

Each section starts with a "Why It Matters" explanation to explain the rationale behind each step. It's followed by "Actionable Steps," which are practical exercises or strategies you can immediately apply. This structure is designed to give you the understanding and tools to build your personal brand effectively.

Here's how you can make the most of this workbook:

Take Your Time: Personal branding is not a race. It's a process of introspection, discovery, and action. Take your time to reflect on each exercise, and don't rush the process.

Be Honest: The power of a personal brand comes from its authenticity. Be honest with yourself during each exercise. It's the best way to create a brand that truly reflects you.

Take Action: Each section includes actionable steps. Don't skip these. The real value of this workbook lies in applying what you've learned. Create a document in your preferred medium, use the exercises and questions, mold your brand, and later modify and develop it further.

Refer Back Often: This workbook is not meant to be read once and forgotten. Keep it handy, and revisit it often. As you grow and evolve, so will your personal brand. Regularly review and update your personal brand to keep it relevant and authentic.

Use the Checklist and Resources: The Personal Branding Checklist in the appendices is a helpful tool to ensure you take the necessary steps in your personal branding journey. The resources list is there to provide you with additional reading and learning materials.

Remember, creating a personal brand is not about crafting a persona or packaging yourself to sell to the world. It's about discovering your authentic self and finding the best way to express that to the world.

It's about aligning your actions with your values, showcasing your unique value, and building meaningful connections with others.

So, prepare to embark on an exciting journey of self-discovery, growth, and empowerment. It's time to let the world see the authentic, unique, and incredible person you are.

Here's to your personal branding journey!

THOMAS ALLAN

EMPOWERING LEADERSHIP, ELEVATING PROFITS:
YOUR NEXT LEVEL IN BUSINESS EXCELLENCE
THE MAGNETIC MINDSET BLOG

Chapter One

Why Personal Branding Matters

In our increasingly connected digital age, you're not just competing with people in your locale, but potentially, with the world. Personal branding is no longer optional whether you're a business owner, a professional, or a job seeker. It's crucial to distinguish yourself from the competition, establish credibility, and expand your reach.

For example, consider Elon Musk, the CEO of SpaceX and Tesla. His brand as a forward-thinking innovator isn't just separate from his businesses—it's integrated and crucial to their success. His online presence and transparent communication style contribute significantly to the perception and popularity of his companies.

A solid personal brand can do more than help you stand out—it can also open doors. For instance, Sheryl Sandberg, the COO of Facebook, utilized her personal brand to initiate meaningful conversations about women in leadership roles with her book "Lean In." Her brand elevated her professional status and allowed her to create a social impact.

Actionable Steps:

1. Self-Reflection: Dedicate time to identifying your core values, strengths, and passions. This self-awareness forms the foundation of your personal brand. Write down what you believe in, what you stand for, and what you do better or differently than others.

What do you believe in?

What do you stand for?

What you do better or differently than others?

2. Online Presence Audit: Review your current online presence. Google yourself and observe the results. Are you projected the way you want to be seen? Are your professional achievements readily available and noteworthy? This can guide you on what needs to be updated, removed, or enhanced.

Are you projected the way you want to be seen?

Are your professional achievements readily available and noteworthy?

What needs to be updated, removed, or enhanced?

3. Define Your Personal Brand: Outline your personal brand based on your self-reflection and audit. This should include your mission (what you aim to achieve), your vision (how you envision your future), and your unique selling proposition (what sets you apart).

Your mission (what you aim to achieve)?

Your vision (how you envision your future)?

Your Unique Selling Proposition (USP) - what sets you apart?

4. Craft Your Personal Brand Statement: This is a concise declaration about your unique value proposition. A solid personal brand statement can capture your identity and professional purpose in a brief sentence or two. Remember to make it clear, powerful, and compelling.

My Personal Brand Statement (you will further refine this as the book goes on, so just have a go – this is your starting point):

5. Plan Your Personal Brand Strategy: Map out a strategy to communicate and develop your brand. This could include launching a personal website, writing articles or blog posts, attending networking events, or giving public speeches. Always ensure that your communications and actions align with your personal brand statement.

With these steps, you're on your way to crafting a robust personal brand that can be a powerful tool in your professional arsenal.

What will you do to develop your brand?

Your Current Role and Your Aspired Role

Why It Matters: Your personal brand isn't just a reflection of who you are now; it's a projection of who you aspire to become. It's a visionary depiction of your potential, which can powerfully influence your professional trajectory. It can help you stand out in your current role, showcasing your skills, attitudes, and values uniquely and compellingly. It can also act as a bridge toward your aspired role by aligning your present image with the skills, experiences, and attributes desired in that future position.

An illustrative example can be found in the career of Oprah Winfrey. She started her career as a news anchor, which was her current role. But she had bigger aspirations—she wanted to connect with people, to have conversations that matter, and to make an impact. She built her brand around these aspirations, which eventually led her to host the globally recognized "The Oprah Winfrey Show." Her brand evolved with her, always aligning with her current roles and future aspirations.

Actionable Steps:

1. Identify Your Current and Aspired Role: Write down the skills, experiences, and attributes associated with your current and aspired roles. Reflect on the commonalities and differences.

Write down the skills, experiences, and attributes associated with your current and role:

Write down the skills, experiences, and attributes associated with your aspired role:

What are the commonalities and differences?

2. Define Your Skills and Values: Identify your skills and values that will serve you well in your aspired role. These can become key elements of your personal brand.

What skills and values will serve you well in your aspired role?

3. Address Skill Gaps: Recognize any skills or experiences you need to develop or acquire to advance into your aspired role. Create a development plan to bridge these gaps over time.

What skills or experiences do you need to develop or acquire to advance into your aspired role?

How will you bridge these gaps over time?

4. Align Your Personal Brand with Your Aspirations: Start projecting yourself in your aspired role. This could mean sharing content related to your future career, engaging in conversations around topics relevant to your aspired role, or even changing your title on LinkedIn to reflect the position you aspire to.

What will you do right now to align your personal brand with your aspirations?

5. Continuous Learning and Development: Regularly review your brand and update it as your skills and career aspirations evolve. Continuously seek learning opportunities that will help you get closer to your aspired role.

Remember, your personal brand should not just mirror who you are at present—it should also illuminate the path to your future, leading you to your aspired role. By taking these actionable steps, you're proactively shaping your career trajectory and opening up new opportunities.

Take some time to schedule your reviews into your diary/planner

Who can you use moving forward as a mentor to check if you are being consistent with your brand?

The Power of Communication

Why It Matters: Communication is the vehicle that conveys your personal brand to the world. It's how you articulate your values, express your personality, and demonstrate your expertise. Effective communication enhances your brand by making you more approachable, relatable, and trustworthy. Conversely, ineffective communication can distort your brand, confuse your audience, and damage your reputation.

One example of a leader who mastered the art of communication is Steve Jobs, co-founder of Apple. Jobs' clear, persuasive, and passionate communication resonated with audiences and played an instrumental role in building his and Apple's corporate brands. His presentations were so influential they became known as the "Reality Distortion Field."

In contrast, poor communication can harm your personal brand, as exemplified by various CEOs who mishandled crisis communications, which led to a decline in their reputation, and in some cases, even their resignation.

"The art of communication is the language of leadership."[1]

Actionable Steps:

1. Evaluate Your Communication Skills: Reflect on your current communication style and skills. Do you communicate clearly and confidently? Are you adept at listening? Do you manage to convey your thoughts effectively, both in writing and speech? Identify areas that need improvement.

Do you communicate clearly and confidently? Are you adept at listening? Do you manage to convey your thoughts effectively, both in writing and speech? (A good opportunity to get feedback from others too)

Identify areas that need improvement:

2. Develop Your Personal Brand's Voice: Your voice reflects your brand personality. Is your brand professional, friendly, inspirational, or humorous? Your voice should be consistent across all platforms and forms of communication.

Is your brand professional, friendly, inspirational, or humorous?

Check all platforms where your brand and voice is present. What do you need to change to make it consistent?

3. Craft Your Personal Brand Story: Stories captivate and engage people. Create a compelling narrative that shares your journey, mission, and what sets you apart. This story can be a powerful tool for communicating your brand.

Create a compelling narrative that shares your journey, mission, and what sets you apart.

4. Practice Articulating Your Personal Brand: Whether it's a job interview, a networking event, or a social media post, be prepared to communicate your brand succinctly and effectively. This includes having an "elevator pitch" ready—a concise and compelling explanation of who you are, what you do, and why it matters.

Create an "elevator pitch" — a concise and compelling explanation of who you are, what you do, and why it matters. Practice and rehearse until it is embedded. Get feedback.

5. Continual Learning and Improvement: Communication is a skill that can continuously be improved. Seek feedback, invest in training courses, or join groups like Toastmasters to hone your skills.

Remember, your communication skills supplement your personal brand and are an integral part of it. How you communicate should reflect your brand's core values and attributes, further strengthening your authenticity and impact.

What feedback have you received? What else can you do to develop a 'Magnetic Mindset"?

Time to get into it ...

That seems like quite a bit to unpack in just an introductory section, doesn't it? There's a reason for this. I firmly believe in starting any journey with a clear destination in mind. Throughout the subsequent chapters, you will find that some elements of this initial groundwork will be revisited and refined. This isn't redundancy or repetition for its own sake. Instead, it's a purposeful strategy designed to help you critically reassess your initial efforts, build upon them, and polish them until they shine.

This methodology will guide you into a more granular exploration of personal branding, ultimately helping you cultivate a robust and compelling personal brand that can be seamlessly incorporated into your business or professional persona. Since you've now practiced these foundational elements, you will likely find that some of the answers will come to you more readily. And if they don't, that's perfectly fine - it's all part of the process.

This approach has proven highly effective in my coaching sessions with executives and individuals preparing for interviews. With a polished personal brand, you will be prepared to respond to various questions or scenarios consistently and authentically, no matter how they are framed.

As we proceed, you will notice specific themes and questions reoccurring, albeit in different forms. This isn't merely to challenge your initial brand identification. Rather, it's intended to engrain your personal brand so deeply within you that it becomes an integral part of your identity.

Chapter Two

Discovering Your Personal Brand

Personal Brand Assessment

The Deep Dive: To establish a solid and authentic personal brand, you need to engage in deep introspection. This personal brand assessment is designed to guide you in uncovering your core strengths, values, passions, and aspirations. It's an opportunity to uncover what makes you unique and how you can leverage these qualities to stand out and achieve your professional goals.

For example, Howard Schultz, the former CEO of Starbucks, attributes the company's focus on community and human connection to his values and experiences. His brand and Starbucks' corporate brand are closely intertwined, illustrating how understanding and leveraging one's values can shape both individual and organizational success.

Actionable Steps:

1. Identify Your Core Strengths: Consider what you excel at. What are the skills or talents that set you apart from others? What have others complimented you on or sought your help with? These can be technical skills, like proficiency in particular software, or soft skills, like leadership or problem-solving.

Write down at least five strengths you possess.

1.

2.

3.

4.

5.

What are the skills or talents that set you apart from others?

What have others complimented you on or sought your help with?

2. Define Your Values: What principles or standards guide your life? What do you believe in? What are you unwilling to compromise on? Identifying your values can help you ensure that your brand aligns with what is most important to you.

What principles or standards guide your life?

What do you believe in?

What are you unwilling to compromise on?

3. Discover Your Passions: What do you love to do? What activities make you lose track of time? What topics can you spend hours discussing? Recognizing your passions can add depth and authenticity to your brand, making it more relatable and engaging.

What do you love to do?

What activities make you lose track of time?

What topics can you spend hours discussing?

4. Outline Your Aspirations: What are your professional goals? What kind of career would you like to have? Where do you see yourself in five, ten, or fifteen years? Understanding your aspirations can help you align your brand with your career objectives, making it a tool that aids your professional advancement.

What are your professional goals?

What kind of career would you like to have?

Where do you see yourself in five years?

Where do you see yourself in ten years?

Where do you see yourself in fifteen years?

5. Compile Your Personal Brand Assessment: Bring together your strengths, values, passions, and aspirations to start forming your brand. Look for patterns, overlaps, and points of synergy. The intersection of these elements often forms the core of your personal brand.

Remember, your brand should be a true reflection of who you are. It should encapsulate your strengths, passions, and values while aligning with your professional aspirations. This personal brand assessment lays the foundation for building a solid and genuine personal brand.

Compile Your Personal Brand Assessment:

The Personal Brand Statement

Crafting Your Signature: Your personal brand statement is a concise, powerful expression of your professional identity. It encapsulates your unique value proposition, combining who you are, what you do, and how you do it. An effective personal brand statement can distinguish you from the competition, make a strong impression, and leave a lasting memory.

Consider Richard Branson, the founder of the Virgin Group. His personal brand statement might be something like: "An adventurous entrepreneur dedicated to challenging conventions and creating innovative solutions that change lives."

Actionable Steps:

1. Identify Your Unique Value Proposition: Reflect on what makes you different from others in your field. This could be a unique combination of skills, experiences, or perspectives. It might also be a distinctive approach you take to your work.

What is your Unique value Proposition (USP)?

2. Define Your Target Audience: Determine who you want to connect with through your brand. This could be potential employers, clients, or industry peers. Understanding your audience can help you tailor your brand statement to resonate with them.

Define Your Target Audience:

3. Combine Your Identity, Value, and Audience: Your brand statement should briefly articulate who you are, what unique value you offer, and whom you serve. Use clear and compelling language that reflects your personal brand's voice.

Combine Your Identity, Value, and Audience:

4. Write Your Personal Brand Statement: Based on these elements, write your brand statement. It should be no more than one to two sentences long. Remember, this is your "elevator pitch"—a succinct and impactful statement that encapsulates your personal brand.

Write Your Personal Brand Statement:

5. Test and Refine Your Statement: Share your brand statement with trusted friends, mentors, or colleagues. Ask for their feedback. Does it accurately represent you? Is it compelling? Refine your statement based on the feedback you receive.

An example to get you started might look like this: "I am a creative and dedicated marketing professional with a unique ability to understand consumer needs and translate them into innovative strategies that drive business growth."

Remember, your brand statement should be an authentic and memorable representation of who you are professionally. Take time to craft, test, and refine it until it resonates with your identity and aspirations.

Your Unique Selling Proposition (USP)

Stand Out from the Crowd: Your Unique Selling Proposition, or USP, is a specific, clear, and concise statement communicating why you are different from and superior to others in your field. Your USP makes you stand out and can be the deciding factor for a potential employer or client choosing you over a competitor.

Think about Sara Blakely, the founder of Spanx. Her USP could be: "As a self-made billionaire entrepreneur, I turned my frustration with undergarments into a revolutionary product that transformed the apparel industry."

Actionable Steps:

1. Review Your Personal Brand Assessment: Refer back to the core strengths, values, and passions you identified in your brand assessment. These can often provide insights into what makes you unique.

2. Research Your Competition: Understanding what others in your field are doing can help you identify what sets you apart. Look at their strengths and weaknesses, and see how to differentiate yourself.

Who is your competition? What are their strengths and weaknesses? How will you differentiate yourself?

3. Identify Your Unique Traits: What unique skills, experiences, or perspectives do you bring to your work? This could be a specialized skill set, a unique background, a fresh approach, or a combination.

What unique skills, experiences, or perspectives do you bring to your work?

4. Test Your USP: Discuss your identified USP with trusted peers, mentors, or coaches. Ask for their honest feedback. Does your USP resonate? Is it truly unique? Refine your USP based on their feedback.

Does your USP resonate? Is it truly unique?

5. Articulate Your USP: Craft a clear and compelling statement that encapsulates your USP. Ensure it aligns with your personal brand statement and overall branding strategy.

Remember, your USP isn't just what you do—it's how you do it differently than anyone else. Your USP should be integral to your brand, highlighting your unique value and making you stand out in a crowded market.

Articulate Your USP: Craft a clear and compelling statement that encapsulates your USP:

Chapter Three

Crafting Your Personal Brand Image

Visual Branding

Why It Matters: Visual branding is vital to your brand image. It creates a visual language that communicates your brand's essence without words. A consistent visual identity helps to establish recognition and recall, making you more memorable in the minds of your audience. Think of Elon Musk; his consistent visual branding across platforms—often characterized by clean, simple designs and powerful imagery—communicates an image of innovation, boldness, and future orientation.

Actionable Steps:

1. Determine Your Personal Brand's Visual Identity: Reflect on the aspects of your brand that you want to highlight visually. This could be your profession- alism, creativity, passion, or sophistication, among other attributes.

Determine Your Personal Brand's Visual Identity:

2. Select Your Brand Colors: Colors evoke emotions and communicate non- verbally. Choose colors that align with your brand attributes. For example, blue often conveys trust and reliability, while green can represent growth and renewal.

Select Your Brand Colors:

3. Choose Your Fonts: Fonts can convey personality. A serif font might com- municate a traditional, reliable, professional image, while a sans-serif font might appear modern and clean. A script font can convey creativity and ele- gance.

What is your font?

4. Profile Pictures and Logos: Have a high-quality, professional profile picture for use across platforms. This enhances your credibility and recognizability. If applicable, consider creating a personal logo that encapsulates your brand (consider using freelance services such as FIVERR or UPWORK to do this for you)

Choose your profile pictures and/o logos that you will use.

5. Maintain Consistency Across Platforms: Use the same profile picture, logo, color scheme, and fonts across all your professional and social platforms. Consistency strengthens brand recognition and trust.

Take time to upload to all platforms your brand is represented on.

6. Update Regularly: As your brand evolves, so should your visual branding. Please review and update your visual brand elements periodically to ensure they continue to reflect your brand accurately.

Set aside time in your diary and planner for review.

Remember, visual branding isn't just about aesthetics—it's a powerful communication tool that speaks volumes about your brand. A consistent and well-thought-out visual identity can make a lasting impression and set you apart from the competition.

Personal Style

Why It Matters: Your personal style and grooming are extensions of your brand and can significantly impact people's perceptions of you. A well-curated personal style can enhance your credibility, express your personality, and even signify your professional competence. Steve Jobs, for instance, was known for his signature black turtleneck, jeans, and sneakers—a uniform that reflected his brand's focus on simplicity and design.

Actionable Steps:

1. Identify Your Brand Attributes: Reflect on the key attributes of your brand. Are you innovative,creative, formal, laid-back, stylish, or traditional? Your personal style should be an embodiment of these attributes.

Identify Your Brand Attributes:

2. Define Your Personal Style: Based on your brand attributes, define your style. This could be professional, creative, minimalistic, chic, or different styles. Remember, your style should align with your industry and the expectations of your target audience.

Define Your Personal Style:

3. Grooming: Good grooming isn't just about looking neat—it's about projecting self-respect and attention to detail. This can include maintaining a well-kept hairstyle, ensuring your clothes are clean and pressed, and adopting good skincare and personal hygiene habits.

Does your grooming match your brand? Should you change anything?

4. Consistency: Like with your visual brand, maintaining a consistent personal style helps build recognition and trust. While it's OK to vary your outfits, maintain a consistent theme that aligns with your brand.

How can you start ensuring consistency?

5. Comfort and Authenticity: While your style should enhance your brand, it should also be comfortable and authentic to who you are. Don't feel pressured to conform to trends or expectations that don't resonate with you.

Are you authentic to your brand?

Remember, your personal style and grooming are silent communicators of your brand. They should be seen as tools that help you express your identity, connect with your target audience, and differentiate yourself in the marketplace.

Creating a Personal Brand Mood Board

Visualizing Your Brand: A personal brand mood board is a visual tool that helps you define and communicate the aesthetic and feel of your brand. It can include colors, typography, imagery, patterns, and textures representing your brand. For example, if Oprah Winfrey were to create a mood board, it might feature images of empowerment, warm and inviting colors, and powerful yet approachable typography.

Actionable Steps:

Define Your Brand Attributes: Refer back to the attributes you identified in your brand assessment. What visuals best represent these traits?

What visuals best represent these traits? (you could use free stock images from Unsplash or Pexels)

Gather Inspirational Visuals: Start gathering images, colors, fonts, quotes, textures, and anything else that visually represents your brand attributes. These can be physical cut-outs from magazines or digital images saved from websites. Tools like Pinterest or Canva can be great resources for this step.

Create a folder for your personal brand

1. Select a Platform: Decide where to create your mood board. This could be a physical board in your workspace or a digital platform like Pinterest, Adobe Spark, or Canva.

2. Arrange Your Mood Board: Arrange your selected visuals on your platform. Group similar colors, textures, and images together to create flow and visual cohesion.

3. Evaluate Your Mood Board: Once you've arranged it, step back and evaluate it. Does it represent your brand? Do the visuals convey the feel and aesthetic you want to be associated with your brand? Make any necessary adjustments.

4. Use Your Mood Board: Refer to your mood board as you make decisions about your brand. This could be when selecting an outfit for a professional event, designing your personal website, or creating content for social media.

Remember, your mood board is a living, breathing representation of your brand. It can evolve and change as your brand does. Use it as a guide and inspiration as you craft and express your brand.

Chapter Four

Communicating Your Personal Brand

Communication Style

Why It Matters: Your communication style is a significant aspect of your brand. It includes expressing your thoughts and feelings, interacting with others, and presenting yourself. It's not just about what you say but how you say it. A strong communication style can increase your influence, improve relationships, and enhance your reputation. Consider figures like Michelle Obama; her communication style is warm, approachable, and inspiring, embodying her personal brand.

Actionable Steps:

1. Assess Your Current Communication Style: Reflect on how you communicate. Are you direct or indirect? Do you prefer written or verbal communication? Do you focus on facts and figures or stories and experiences? Knowing your natural style can help you identify its strengths and potential areas for improvement.

Reflect on how you communicate.

Are you direct or indirect? Do you prefer written or verbal communication? Do you focus on facts and figures or stories and experiences?

2. Identify Your Desired Communication Style: Based on your brand attributes, determine how you want to communicate. If your brand is about being innovative and bold, you might choose a direct, confident, and articulate style. A more empathetic and patient style might be appropriate if your brand is about being supportive and compassionate.

Based on your brand attributes, determine how you want to communicate.

3. Practice Active Listening: Effective communication isn't just about speaking; it's also about listening. Active listening can build trust, foster understanding, and enhance your relationships. Practice active listening by focusing entirely on the speaker, avoiding interruptions, and responding thoughtfully.

Do you actively listen? Do you have a Magnetic Mindset?

4. Embrace Constructive Feedback: Constructive feedback can help you grow and improve. Please take it in stride, whether about your communication style or work. Accept it gracefully and use it to better yourself and your brand.

How well do you accept feedback?

5. Adapt Your Communication Style: Different situations and people may require different communication styles. Be adaptable and flexible, adjusting your style while staying true to your brand.

What situations do you need to change your communication style?

6. Continually Improve: Like any skill, effective communication can be developed over time. Continually seek opportunities to improve and refine your communication skills.

Repetition, like in these exercises, helps engrain your brand. It can be tedious, but the benefits can be exponential for your business and career.

Remember, communication is a cornerstone of your brand. Your communication should reflect who you are and what you stand for. As you build your brand, strive to develop a communication style that is both effective and authentically you.

The Power of Storytelling

Why It Matters: Storytelling is a powerful tool for personal branding. It lets you connect with your audience emotionally, making your brand more memorable and relatable. By telling your story, you provide context, invoke empathy, and make your brand uniquely yours. Consider the story of Howard Schultz, the former CEO of Starbucks. His narrative about growing up in a poor neighborhood and dreaming of creating a company that offered health benefits to all employees, even part-timers, has been integral to Starbucks' brand.

Actionable Steps:

1. Identify Your Personal Stories: Reflect on your experiences representing your brand attributes. These could be stories about overcoming challenges, achieving goals, learning lessons, or personal growth.

What personal stories will enhance your brand?

2. Structure Your Story: A compelling story often has a clear structure: a beginning that sets the stage, a middle that introduces conflict or a challenge, and an end that brings resolution and insight.

Develop your story: beginning, middle and end:

3. Make It Relatable: To resonate with your audience, your story needs to be relatable. This doesn't mean it needs to be ordinary—instead, focus on the emotions, challenges, and triumphs that most people can identify with.

Does your story resonate?

4. Share Your Story: Integrate your story into personal branding communications. This could be in your 'About Me' section on your website, during a job interview, in your social media posts, or public speeches or presentations.

Update your 'About Me' sections on all relevant platforms.

5. Consistency: Ensure your stories are consistent with your brand and reinforce the image you want to project.

Rehearse your story so it flows naturally and consistently.

6. Authenticity: Be genuine in your storytelling. Authentic stories tend to engage audiences more and build stronger connections.

Can you make it even more authentic? Acknowledging mistakes and lessons learnt can add power to your story.

Remember, storytelling in personal branding isn't just about self-promotion—it's about sharing your journey, lessons, and values. Well-crafted stories can give your audience valuable insights into who you are, not just what you've done, making your brand more compelling and memorable.

Chapter Five

Bringing Your Personal Brand to Life

Digital Presence

Why It Matters: In today's digital age, your online presence is often the first point of contact between you and potential employers, clients, or collaborators. Whether through social media, blogs, podcasts, or your website, these digital platforms give you a stage to showcase your brand to a global audience. They also allow you to control and manage your reputation, demonstrate your expertise, and engage with your audience. Consider Elon Musk: his Twitter presence, while sometimes controversial, has undeniably played a significant role in his brand, amplifying his image as a forward-thinking and outspoken tech innovator.

Actionable Steps:

1. Choose Your Platforms: Not all digital platforms suit you or your brand. Choose those that align with your brand attributes and where your target audience spends their time. LinkedIn, for example, is excellent for professional networking, while Instagram might be a better fit for visually-oriented brands.

Choose Your Platforms that fit your brand:

Do you need to get rid of platforms that are inconsistent with your brand?

2. Create a Consistent Profile: Consistency is vital in personal branding. Use a professional and recognizable profile picture across all your digital platforms. Your biography should be concise, clear, and consistent, effectively communicating your brand.

Create a concise, clear, and consistent biography, effectively communicating your brand.

3. Develop a Content Strategy: What content will you share? This could in-clude blog posts, videos, photos, podcasts, or infographics. Whatever form it takes, your content should offer value to your audience and reflect your brand.

What content will you share?

4. Engage with Your Audience: Interaction is a significant advantage of digital platforms. Engage with your followers by responding to comments, partici-pating in discussions, and showing appreciation for their support.

Choose Your Platforms that fit your brand:

Repetition, like in these exercises, helps engrain your brand. It can be tedious, but the benefits can be exponential for your business and career.

5. Monitor Your Online Reputation: Regularly google your name and set up Google Alerts to stay informed of any online mentions. This will allow you to manage your online reputation and ensure it aligns with your brand.

Choose Your Platforms that fit your brand:

6. Continue Learning and Adapting: Digital trends change rapidly. Stay informed about new platforms,strategies, or changes impacting your digital presence.

Remember, your digital presence is an extension of your brand. It's not just about being present on digital platforms—it's about leveraging them to communicate your brand, engage with your audience, and achieve your professional goals.

Networking

Why It Matters: Networking can be crucial in developing and reinforcing your brand. It can allow you to establish valuable connections, share your expertise, gain insights, and increase your visibility— additionally, the impression you make. At the same time, networking can significantly impact how others perceive your brand. For instance, Reid Hoffman, co-founder of LinkedIn, is known for his net-work- intelligent approach, which played a significant role in his success, making him a living representation of the brand he helped to create.

Actionable Steps:

1. Identify Relevant Networking Events: Look for industry-specific events, local business meetings, conferences, or online networking forums that align with your brand and where you can connect with key players in your field.

Identify Relevant Networking Events:

2. Prepare Your Introduction: A short, compelling introduction encapsulates your brand. It should be conversational and engaging, giving others a clear sense of who you are and what you do.

Prepare Your Introduction:

3. Focus on Building Relationships: Networking is about building relationships, not just distributing business cards. Show genuine interest in others, ask questions, and look for ways you can provide value.

Focus on Building Relationships - do you have a Magnetic Mindset?:

4. Share Your Brand Story: Use your brand story to engage and connect with others on a deeper level. Stories can be more memorable and impactful than facts alone.

Rehearse your brand story to help you connect deeply.

5. Follow Up: Follow up with the contacts you made after the event. Send a personalized note mentioning something you discussed or expressing appreciation for their time.

How will you follow-up? How will you ask if you can follow-up?

6. Leverage Social Media: Social media platforms like LinkedIn can be effective for continuing the relationships you build in person. Connect with the people you meet, share relevant content, and engage with their posts.

Are there people in your network you have not connected with? Why? How and when will you?

7. Be Consistent: Ensure that the image you project while networking is consistent with your overall personal brand. All elements should align with your brand, from your appearance to your communication style.

Once again, do a check across all platforms. Are you consistent?

Remember, networking is a two-way street. As much as it is about conveying your brand, it's also about listening, learning, and building genuine connections. Approach each networking opportunity with an open mind and clear understanding of your brand.

Creating a Personal Brand Website

Why It Matters: A personal brand website can significantly boost your online presence. It serves as a hub for all information about you and your brand, showcasing your portfolio, skills, experiences, and anything else that adds to your brand's story. Moreover, unlike social media platforms, it gives you complete control over your narrative. For instance, renowned marketing expert Seth Godin maintains a personal blog that effectively communicates his insights, authority, and unique brand to his audience.

If you do not have the skills or time, consider outsourcing this section. Freelancers can be surprisingly cheap, have better skills, and be quicker at developing this. You can provide all the necessary information below to ensure it aligns with your brand requirements, and you can even outsource blog posts for your content and use AI platforms.

Actionable Steps:

1. **Choose a Domain Name:** Your domain name should ideally be your name or something that relates closely to your brand. It should be easy to spell and remember.

2. **Select a Platform:** Use a website builder platform that aligns with your technical abilities and requirements. WordPress, Wix, and Squarespace are popular choices that offer a variety of templates.

3. **Design Your Website:** Ensure your website design is consistent with your brand, including your color scheme, fonts, and overall style. Make it clean, professional, and easy to navigate.

4. **About Me Page:** This is where your brand statement and story come into play. Write compelling content that communicates who you are, what you do, and how you can provide value.

5. **Showcase Your Work:** Include a portfolio, case studies, or testimonials that showcase your skills, experiences, and successes. If possible, pro-

vide quantifiable results.

6. **Include a Blog or Resources:** Sharing relevant content can demonstrate your expertise and provide value to your audience. This can be blog posts, articles, guides, tools, or links to your podcasts or video content.

7. **Contact Information:** Make it easy for visitors to contact you. Include your professional email address and, if applicable, links to your social media profiles.

8. **SEO Optimization:** Use SEO best practices to improve your website's visibility on search engines. This includes using relevant keywords, creating quality content, and ensuring your site is mobile-friendly.

9. **Update Regularly:** Keep your website updated with your latest work, insights, and experiences. An updated website can help maintain your audience's interest and attract more visitors.

10. **Analytics:** Use tools like Google Analytics to understand your website's traffic and visitor behavior. This can help you make necessary adjustments to enhance your experience.

Having your personal brand website can significantly enhance your online presence and visibility, allowing you to reach a wider audience and opening up new opportunities.

Chapter Six

Aligning Your Personal Brand with Your Business or Role

Defining Your Professional Brand

Why It Matters: Your professional brand is essentially an extension of your brand within a professional context. It encapsulates your professional roles, skills, values, and contributions. When your professional brand aligns with your brand, it creates a strong, cohesive image that enhances your credibility and authenticity. Take Steve Jobs, for example; his professional brand as an innovative, detail-oriented leader perfectly matched his brand, reinforcing his reputation and credibility.

Actionable Steps:

1. Identify Your Professional Values: What values drive you in your professional life? These could be things like integrity, innovation, or customer satisfaction. Your professional values should align with your values.

What values drive you in your professional life?

2. Define Your Professional Roles: Are you a leader, a team player, a creative thinker, or a problem-solver? Define the roles you play in your professional life that align with your brand.

Are you a leader, a team player, a creative thinker, or a problem-solver?

3. Identify Your Skills and Strengths: What skills and strengths set you apart in your field? Maybe you're a talented coder, a skilled negotiator, or a gifted speaker. These skills should support and enhance your brand.

What skills and strengths set you apart in your field?

4. Define Your Unique Professional Contributions: What unique contributions do you make in your professional field? Perhaps you bring innovative ideas, deliver high-quality results, or build strong relationships.

What unique contributions do you make in your professional field?

5. Create a Professional Brand Statement: Your professional brand statement should encapsulate your roles, skills, values, and unique contributions. It should be consistent with your brand statement and communicate what you bring professionally.

Create a Professional Brand Statement:

6. Communicate Your Professional Brand: Use your professional brand statement in your LinkedIn profile, resume, and professional settings. Consistently communicate your professional brand in all professional interactions.

Communicate Your Professional Brand – Practice!:

7. Live Your Professional Brand: Ensure your actions, decisions, and work quality reflect your professional brand. This consistency between your brand and your actions will enhance your credibility and reputation.

Once again, do a check across all platforms. Are you consistent?

Remember, aligning your professional brand with your brand can enhance your reputation, differentiate you in your field, and open doors to opportunities that align with your personal and professional goals. It helps you to not only talk the talk but walk the walk.

Bridging the Gap

Why It Matters: Sometimes, there can be a gap between your brand and your professional brand. This can create a disjointed image and confuse your audience or potential employers. Bridging this gap allows for a more cohesive, authentic representation of who you are, personally and professionally. This alignment builds trust and ensures you are attracting the right opportunities and connections that resonate with your whole self.

Actionable Steps:

1. Identify the Gaps: Start by conducting a self-assessment. Identify where inconsistencies between your personal and professional brands exist. Are there values you uphold personally that aren't reflected in your work? Do your personal interests and passions align with your professional pursuits?

Identify where inconsistencies between your personal and professional brands exist:

2. Realign Your Values: It may be time to realign if your professional life doesn't reflect your values. This might mean prioritizing projects that better reflect your values or even seeking out new roles or companies that resonate with your personal beliefs.

Do you need to realign?

3. Incorporate Your Personality: Don't keep your personal and professional life completely separate. Let your personality shine through in your professional brand. This unique personality can often differentiate you from others in your field.

Does your personality shine through?

4. Develop New Skills: If your brand emphasizes a skill that isn't currently part of your professional brand, take steps to develop that skill in a professional context. This could involve seeking further education, asking for new responsibilities at work, or finding a mentor.

What new skills are required, if any?

5. Communicate Effectively: Consistently communicate the alignment of your personal and professional brands. This could be in your "About Me" section on LinkedIn, in a cover letter, or during a job interview.

Another check - consistency is imperative.

6. Walk Your Talk: Make sure that your actions reflect the alignment of your personal and professional brands. This includes the work you do, how you interact with others, and how you handle challenges.

Do your actions align with your personal and professional brands? Do you need to change anything?

Remember, bridging the gap between your personal and professional brand is not about creating a facade or being someone you're not. It's about ensuring that all aspects of your brand authentically reflect your values, strengths, passions, and goals.

Personal Brand in Action

Why It Matters: Demonstrating your brand in your professional life can significantly enhance your career. It allows you to stand out, show your uniqueness, and build a reputation that precedes you. Successful entrepreneurs like Elon Musk and Jeff Bezos have shown that incorporating their brands into their businesses amplifies their success and creates a loyal following.

Actionable Steps:

1. Communication: Use your unique communication style in professional interactions. This includes emails, meetings, presentations, and networking events. Be consistent and authentic in expressing your ideas and perspectives.

2. Online Presence: Leverage social media platforms and professional networking sites like LinkedIn to communicate your brand consistently. Share content and engage in discussions that reflect your values and areas of expertise.

3. Professional Activities: Choose projects, roles, and initiatives that align with your brand. This allows you to showcase your skills and passions and ensures that you are investing your time and energy in endeavors that you find fulfilling.

4. Mentorship and Leadership: As a leader or mentor, you can express your brand through your leadership style, how you make decisions, how you support your team, and how you handle challenges.

5. Networking: Use networking opportunities to articulate your brand. Have a succinct and compelling personal brand statement ready to share when meeting new people.

6. Continuous Learning: Engage in continuous learning opportunities that align with your brand. This could be attending seminars, gaining new certifications, or reading up on industry trends. This demonstrates your commitment to your brand values and goals.

7. Work Environment and Culture: Your work environment should reflect your brand. Whether it's your personal workspace or the overall company culture, ensuring it aligns with your brand can help you feel more fulfilled and engaged in your work.

8. Problem-solving: Showcase your unique approach to problem-solving in your professional life. This will underline your brand's distinctive characteristics, such as creativity, analytical abilities, and resilience.

Remember, your brand is not something to be switched on and off, depending on the setting. It should be evident in all aspects of your life, particularly in your professional activities. It is a living entity and needs continuous nurturing and manifestation.

Chapter Seven

Maintaining and Growing Your Personal Brand

Regular Assessment

Why It Matters: Much like any brand, your brand is not a static entity. It should evolve as you grow, learn, and gain new experiences. Regular assessment ensures that your brand accurately reflects you and keeps pace with your development. It also helps you stay relevant, connected with your audience, and in control of your narrative. Think of celebrities like Madonna or entrepreneurs like Richard Branson, who've evolved their brands over time while staying true to their core essence.

Actionable Steps:

1. Schedule Regular Assessments: Decide on a timeframe that works for you (quarterly, bi-annually, or annually), and stick to it. Create reminders if necessary.

2. Revisit Your Personal Brand Statement: As you grow and evolve, so might your values, passions, and aspirations. It's essential to ensure your brand statement stays updated and relevant.

3. Collect Feedback: Seek feedback from colleagues, mentors, clients, or other relevant persons who interact with your brand. Ask specific questions about your perceived strengths, areas for improvement, and how well you align with your stated personal brand.

4. Review Your Online Presence: Your online presence is a public projection of your brand. Regularly review your social media profiles, website, blog posts, and other online content to ensure they align with your brand.

5. Assess Your Achievements: Look back at your accomplishments since your last assessment. Have you achieved what you set out to do? Do these achievements reflect your brand?

6. Identify Areas for Development: Look for areas where you could improve or enhance your brand. Do you need to work on your public speaking skills? Should you be more active on social media?

7. Update Your Goals: Based on your assessment, update your personal and professional goals. Remember, your brand should help you achieve these goals.

8. Create an Action Plan: Based on the insights from your assessment, create an action plan. This might involve taking a course, attending a seminar, revamping your website, or creating new networking opportunities.

Remember, maintaining and growing your brand is an ongoing process. Regular assessment and refinement ensure your brand stays fresh, relevant, and true to who you are.

Overcoming Challenges

Why It Matters: Personal branding, like any journey, is not always smooth sailing. Sometimes, you may face a crisis or challenge that threatens to damage your personal brand. This could range from a public failure to a social media mishap. How you handle these situations can significantly affect your brand image. Overcoming challenges and crises with grace, humility, and resilience can strengthen your brand. A good example is how Starbucks CEO Kevin Johnson swiftly apologized and took corrective action when a racial bias incident occurred in one of their stores.

Actionable Steps:

1. Stay Calm: In the face of a personal brand crisis, the first step is to stay calm. Take time to understand the situation thoroughly before you react.

2. Assess the Situation: Identify the crisis's source and potential impact on your brand. Is it a mistake you've made, a misunderstanding, or an external event that's out of your control?

3. Acknowledge and Apologize: If the crisis was due to your error or misjudgment, acknowledge it publicly. Apologize sincerely and take full responsibility. The public generally appreciates honesty and humility.

4. Correct Misinformation: If the crisis arose from a misunderstanding or misinformation, politely correct it. Provide accurate information and try to steer the conversation toward the truth.

5. Take Corrective Action: Demonstrate your commitment to your values and integrity by taking appropriate action to rectify the situation. This could be changing a behavior, making amends, or implementing new measures to prevent similar incidents.

6. Seek Support: Reach out to your mentors, colleagues, or PR experts if the situation is severe. They can provide valuable advice and guidance on how to manage the crisis.

7. Learn from the Experience: Every crisis is a learning opportunity. Reflect on what led to the crisis, how you handled it, and how you can prevent similar incidents in the future.

8. Rebuild Trust: Depending on the severity of the crisis, rebuilding trust might take time. Be consistent in showing your values and commitment. Over time, your actions will speak louder than the crisis.

Remember, handling crises effectively can show your ability to take responsibility, your strength of character, and your commitment to your brand. It can turn a negative situation into an opportunity for personal growth and brand strengthening.

Evolving Your Brand

Why It Matters: Just as people grow and change over time, so should their brand. A personal brand that reflects your current aspirations, skills, and experiences is more authentic and relevant. This evolution is a natural process and shows your audience that you are growing professionally and as an individual. Successful individuals like Oprah Winfrey have demonstrated this beautifully as her brand evolved from talk show host to philanthropist and global influencer.

Actionable Steps:

1. Stay Self-Aware: Keep in tune with your changing interests, skills, and goals. Self-reflection and introspection are key to understanding how you evolve as a person and professional.

2. Embrace Change: Don't be afraid to pivot and adapt your brand to reflect your current self better. Embracing change can bring fresh energy and relevance to your brand.

3. Consistent Learning: Seek out new learning opportunities and experiences. Gaining new skills, expanding your knowledge, and exploring new interests can all influence the evolution of your brand.

4. Update Your Branding Elements: As your brand evolves, so should the elements that communicate it. This could include your brand statement, visual identity, online presence, and communication style.

5. Engage With Your Network: Keep your network informed about the evolution of your brand. Sharing your growth journey can strengthen relationships and open new opportunities.

6. Seek Feedback: Regularly ask for feedback from your network. This can provide valuable insights into how others perceive your brand and where you might need adjustments.

Remember, evolving your personal brand doesn't mean losing your core identity. It's about growing and adapting your brand to reflect your current self while maintaining the values and principles that define you. This continual evolution can keep your personal brand vibrant, relevant, and true to who you are.

Chapter Eight

Final Thoughts

Why It Matters: Our brand is more than just a marketing tool. It reflects who we are, what we stand for, and the value we bring to the world. Cultivating and nurturing a personal brand is an ongoing journey, not a one-time event. But this journey can be transformative, opening doors to new opportunities, strengthening relationships, and enabling personal and professional growth.

Personal branding has become more critical than ever in today's digital age. Whether we like it or not, we all have a personal brand. The question is whether we consciously shape and guide it or leave it to be defined by others and by circumstance.

Through the steps outlined in this workbook, you have the power to take control of your brand. But knowing is not enough - taking action is critical. Implement the steps, make the necessary adjustments, and continuously nurture and evolve your brand.

Remember, your personal brand is a living, breathing entity. Like any other form of growth, it involves exploration, learning, occasional missteps, and continuous evolution. It's a journey of self-discovery and expression, an ongoing dialogue with yourself and the world.

Embrace this journey with an open mind and heart. Let your brand genuinely reflect you - unique, authentic, and powerful. This is not just about career advancement or business growth - it's about making your mark in the world in a way that's uniquely and authentically you.

So, take the first step today. Start crafting your personal brand and let it be your guiding light on the path to success. Remember, the world needs only the unique blend of talents, skills, and experiences you can offer. Your brand is your gift to the world - let it shine!

Also By Thomas Allan

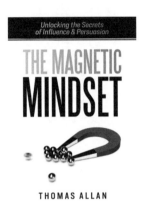

The Magnetic Mindset: Unlocking the Secrets of Influence and Persuasion

Whether you're in a leadership role, looking to ascend the career ladder, or simply desire to have a stronger influence on those around you, this book is your golden ticket.

Featured as **#1 Amazon Hot New Release** in Sales & Selling Management.

Learn from an expert how to go beyond mere selling to **genuinely connect with people.**

Discover the **blend of psychology, communication, and real-life application** that makes the Magnetic Mindset unique.

Neuroleadership: The Science Behind Exceptional Business Leadership

Effective leadership isn't just about strategic decisions and management skills; **it's about truly understanding the intricacies of the human brain.**

Profit Hacking: Strategies for Explosive Profit Growth in the Modern Business Business World

This book isn't just theory; it's a collection of battle-tested strategies and tools frequently compared to the insights in top entrepreneur books. What sets it apart is its no-nonsense, actionable approach that empowers you to implement effective Lead-to-Revenue Management (L2RM) strategies from Day 1.

BRANDING BRILLIANCE

Your Blueprint
to Creating & Communicating an
Irresistible Personal Brand

THOMAS ALLAN

Branding Brilliance: Your Blueprint to Creating & Communicating an Irresistible Personal Brand

In today's digital world, personal branding is no longer optional. We all have a personal brand, whether or not we are aware of it. It's how the world sees us and can significantly impact our careers and lives. This **workbook** is designed to guide you through the process of creating a personal brand that truly reflects who you are and what you stand for.

https://magnet-mind.com/book

in

https://magnet-mind.com/linkedin

Afterword

Your input and feedback through reviews are tremendously important. They guide others in their decision to explore this book. If you've found fresh insights, been led to reconsider your perspectives, discovered practical actions for change, or affirmed your current effective practices, we invite you to share your experiences in a review. Your endorsement would mean the world to us, so if you can spare 5 minutes, I would truly appreciate it. I can't thank you enough for your support and your role in this book's success - you make a big difference!

If you found value in this book and want to further your learning journey, I regularly share thoughts on leadership, mindset, and business on my blog. You're more than welcome to subscribe and join our community: https://magneticmindsetblog.com/

Finally, I am grateful for your commitment, both in reading this book and sharing your thoughts. Your involvement is priceless in ensuring the sustained growth of the Magnetic Mindset Leadership. We're excited to hear from you!

With gratitude, Thomas Allan

About Author

Thomas Allan

Hello, I'm Thomas Allan, an author, executive coach, blogger, and influencer with a diverse and rich professional background. My career, spanning over three decades, has seen me thrive as a psychologist, a senior sales and marketing leader, a consultant, and a business owner. At the heart of my journey has been a deep commitment to leadership development and revenue optimization.

My professional path began in psychology, where I developed a profound understanding of human behavior and mindset. This knowledge has been the cornerstone of my advocacy for a growth mindset. Building on this foundation, I ventured into sales and marketing leadership, driving revenue across various industries. My expertise in pricing strategy, inventory management, and demand forecasting has been instrumental in this success.

I then expanded my horizons to become a consultant and business owner, offering strategic advice and direction to organizations globally. My focus has been on empowering these entities to realize their potential and maximize profitability.

As an author, I've published 'The Magnetic Mindset: Unlocking the Secrets of Influence & Persuasion', 'Profit Hacking: Unlocking Revenue, Maximizing Profit, Get the Lead and Keep the Lead! Strategies for Explosive Profit Growth in the Modern Business World', and 'Branding Brilliance: Your Blueprint to Creating & Communicating an Irresistible Personal Brand'. These works, along with my upcoming series on 'Getting Rich with Passive Income' and 'The Anxiety Advantage: How to Harness Your Nerves for Success in Business', reflect my extensive experience and offer practical steps for effective leadership and profit growth.

In my role as an executive coach, I continue to guide leaders around the world, inspiring them to embrace a growth mindset and enhance their leadership skills. I have a special passion for assisting small business owners in understanding the keys to success in today's business world.

Through my weekly blog at https://magneticmindsetblog.com, I share insights on mindset development, leadership, and profit optimization, reaching a growing audience.

I am Thomas Allan, a multifaceted professional dedicated to inspiring and empowering individuals and organizations. My influence extends beyond my writings, impacting those I coach and consult with, helping them succeed both personally and professionally in today's dynamic business environment.

Join the conversation at: https://magneticmindsetblog.com/

Appendices

Personal Branding Checklist

To ensure that you've taken all the necessary steps in crafting, communicating, and maintaining your personal brand, refer to this checklist:

- Performed a personal brand assessment.

- Defined your personal brand statement.

- Identified your unique selling proposition.

- Established a consistent visual brand across all platforms.

- Develop a personal style that aligns with your brand.

- Created a personal brand mood board.

- Determined your communication style.

- Mastered the art of storytelling for your brand.

- Practiced articulating your brand.

- Established a strong digital presence.

- Leveraged networking events and opportunities for your brand.

- Created a personal brand website.

- Defined your professional brand and aligned it with your personal brand.

- Bridged any gaps between your personal and professional brands.

- Demonstrate your brand in your professional life.

- Regularly evaluated and refined your brand.

- Overcome personal brand challenges or crises.

- Allowed your brand to evolve as you grow professionally and personally.

Printed in France by Amazon
Brétigny-sur-Orge, FR

18310099R00047